Table of contents

I0469667

This information was prepared by the Board of Governors of the Federal Reserve System and the Office of Thrift Supervision in consultation with the following organizations:

AARP
American Association of Residential Mortgage Regulators
America's Community Bankers
Center for Responsible Lending
Conference of State Bank Supervisors
Consumer Federation of America
Consumer Mortgage Coalition
Consumers Union
Credit Union National Association
Federal Deposit Insurance Corporation
Federal Reserve Board's Consumer Advisory Council
Federal Trade Commission
Financial Services Roundtable
Independent Community Bankers Association
Mortgage Bankers Association
Mortgage Insurance Companies of America
National Association of Federal Credit Unions
National Association of Home Builders
National Association of Mortgage Brokers
National Association of Realtors
National Community Reinvestment Coalition
National Consumer Law Center
National Credit Union Administration

This handbook gives you an over-
view of ARMs, explains how ARMs
work, and discusses some of the issues
that you might face as a borrower. It
includes:

- ways to reduce the risks associated with ARMs;
- pointers about advertising and other sources of information, such as lenders and other trusted advisers;
- a glossary of important ARM terms; and
- a worksheet that can help you ask the right questions and figure out whether an ARM is right for you. (Ask lenders to help you fill out the worksheet so you can get the information you need to compare mortgages.)

An adjustable-rate mortgage (ARM) is a loan with an interest
rate that changes. ARMs may start with lower monthly payments
than fixed-rate mortgages, but keep in mind the following:

- Your monthly payments could change. They could go up—sometimes by a lot—even if interest rates don't go up. See page 20.
- Your payments may not go down much, or at all—even if interest rates go down. See page 11.
- You could end up owing more money than you borrowed—even if you make all your payments on time. See page 22.
- If you want to pay off your ARM early to avoid higher payments, you might pay a penalty. See page 24.

You need to compare the features of ARMs to find the one that
best fits your needs. The Mortgage Shopping Worksheet on
page 2 can help you get started.

Mortgage shopping worksheet

Ask your lender or broker to help you fill out this worksheet.

Name of lender or broker and contact information

Mortgage amount

Loan term (e.g., 15 years, 30 years)

Loan description
(e.g., fixed rate, 3/1 ARM, payment-option ARM, interest-only ARM)

Basic Features for Comparison

Fixed-rate mortgage interest rate and annual percentage rate (APR)
(For graduated-payment or stepped-rate mortgages, use the ARM columns.)

ARM initial interest rate and APR
How long does the initial rate apply?

What will the interest rate be after the initial period?

ARM features
How often can the interest rate adjust?

What is the index and what is the current rate? (See chart on page 8.)

What is the margin for this loan?

Interest-rate caps
What is the periodic interest-rate cap?

What is the lifetime interest-rate cap? How high could the rate go?

How low could the interest rate go on this loan?

What is the payment cap?

Can this loan have negative amortization (that is, increase in size)?

What is the limit to how much the balance can grow before the loan will be recalculated?

Is there a prepayment penalty if I pay off this mortgage early?

How long does that penalty last? How much is it?

Is there a balloon payment on this mortgage?
If so, what is the estimated amount and when would it be due?

What are the estimated origination fees and charges for this loan?

Monthly Payment Amounts

What will the monthly payments be for the first year of the loan?

Does this include taxes and insurance? Condo or homeowner's association fees?
If not, what are the estimates for these amounts?

What will my monthly payment be after 12 months if the index rate...
...stays the same?

...goes up 2%?

...goes down 2%?

What is the **most** my minimum monthly payment could be after 1 year?

What is the **most** my minimum monthly payment could be after 3 years?

What is the **most** my minimum monthly payment could be after 5 years?

Fixed-Rate Mortgage	ARM 1	ARM 2	ARM 3

What is an ARM?

An adjustable-rate mortgage differs from a fixed-rate mortgage in many ways. Most importantly, with a fixed-rate mortgage, the interest rate stays the same during the life of the loan. With an ARM, the interest rate changes periodically, usually in relation to an index, and payments may go up or down accordingly.

To compare two ARMs, or to compare an ARM with a fixed-rate mortgage, you need to know about indexes, margins, discounts, caps on rates and payments, negative amortization, payment options, and recasting (recalculating) your loan. You need to consider the maximum amount your monthly payment could increase. Most importantly, you need to know what might happen to your monthly mortgage payment in relation to your future ability to afford higher payments.

Lenders generally charge lower initial interest rates for ARMs than for fixed-rate mortgages. At first, this makes the ARM easier on your pocketbook than would be a fixed-rate mortgage for the same loan amount. Moreover, your ARM could be less expensive over a long period than a fixed-rate mortgage—for example, if interest rates remain steady or move lower.

Against these advantages, you have to weigh the risk that an increase in interest rates would lead to higher monthly payments in the future. It's a trade-off—you get a lower initial rate with an ARM in exchange for assuming more risk over the long run. Here are some questions you need to consider:

- Is my income enough—or likely to rise enough—to cover higher mortgage payments if interest rates go up?

- Will I be taking on other sizable debts, such as a loan for a car or school tuition, in the near future?

- How long do I plan to own this home? (If you plan to sell soon, rising interest rates may not pose the problem they do if you plan to own the house for a long time.)

- Do I plan to make any additional payments or pay the loan off early?

Lenders and Brokers

Mortgage loans are offered by many kinds of lenders—such as banks, mortgage companies, and credit unions. You can also get a loan through a mortgage broker. Brokers "arrange" loans; in other words, they find a lender for you. Brokers generally take your application and contact several lenders, but keep in mind that brokers are not required to find the best deal for you unless they have contracted with you to act as your agent.

How ARMs work: the basic features

Initial rate and payment

The initial rate and payment amount on an ARM will remain in effect for a limited period—ranging from just 1 month to 5 years or more. For some ARMs, the initial rate and payment can vary greatly from the rates and payments later in the loan term. Even if interest rates are stable, your rates and payments could change a lot. If lenders or brokers quote the initial rate and payment on a loan, ask them for the annual percentage rate (APR). If the APR is significantly higher than the initial rate, then it is likely that your rate and payments will be a lot higher when the loan adjusts, even if general interest rates remain the same.

The adjustment period

With most ARMs, the interest rate and monthly payment change every month, quarter, year, 3 years, or 5 years. The period between rate changes is called the *adjustment period*. For example, a loan with an adjustment period of 1 year is called a 1-year ARM, and the interest rate and payment can change once every year; a loan with a 3-year adjustment period is called a 3-year ARM.

Loan Descriptions

Lenders must give you written information on each type of ARM loan you are interested in. The information must include the terms and conditions for each loan, including information about the index and margin, how your rate will be calculated, how often your rate can change, limits on changes (or *caps*), an example of how high your monthly payment might go, and other ARM features such as negative amortization.

The index

The interest rate on an ARM is made up of two parts: the index and the margin. The index is a measure of interest rates generally, and the margin is an extra amount that the lender adds. Your payments will be affected by any caps, or limits, on how high or low your rate can go. If the index rate moves up, so does your interest rate in most circumstances, and you will probably have to make higher monthly payments. On the other hand, if the index rate goes down, your monthly payment could go down. Not all ARMs adjust downward, however—be sure to read the information for the loan you are considering.

Lenders base ARM rates on a variety of indexes. Among the most common indexes are the rates on 1-year constant-maturity Treasury (CMT) securities, the Cost of Funds Index (COFI), and the London Interbank Offered Rate (LIBOR). A few lenders use their own cost of funds as an index, rather than using other indexes. You should ask what index will be used, how it has fluctuated in the past, and where it is published—you can find a lot of this information in major newspapers and on the Internet.

To help you get an idea of how to compare different indexes, the following chart shows a few common indexes over an 11-year period (1996–2008). As you can see, some index rates tend to be higher than others, and some change more often. But if a lender bases interest-rate adjustments on the average value of an index over time, your interest rate would not change as dramatically.

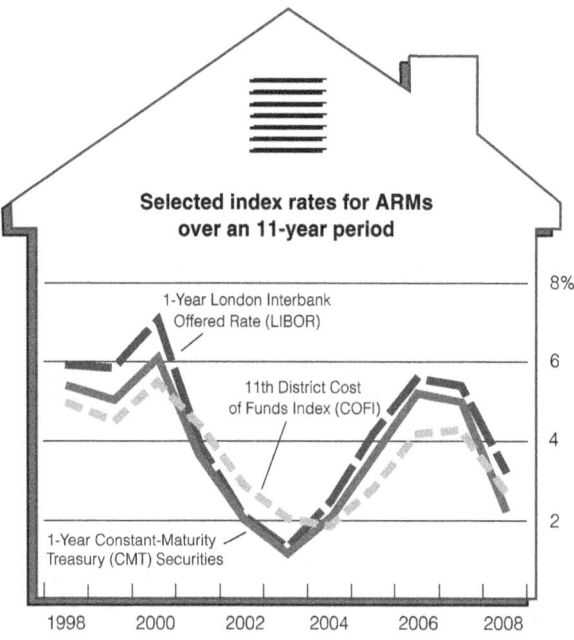

Selected index rates for ARMs over an 11-year period

The margin

To set the interest rate on an ARM, lenders add a few percentage points to the index rate, called the *margin*. The amount of the margin may differ from one lender to another, but it is usually constant over the life of the loan. The *fully indexed rate* is equal to the margin plus the index. If the initial rate on the loan is less than the fully indexed rate, it is called a *discounted index rate*. For example, if the lender uses an index that currently is 4% and adds a 3% margin, the fully indexed rate would be

Index	4%
+ Margin	3%
Fully indexed rate	7%

If the index on this loan rose to 5%, the fully indexed rate would be 8% (5% + 3%). If the index fell to 2%, the fully indexed rate would be 5% (2% + 3%).

Some lenders base the amount of the margin on your credit record— the better your credit, the lower the margin they add—and the lower the interest you will have to pay on your mortgage. In comparing ARMs, look at both the index and margin for each program.

No-Doc/Low-Doc Loans

When you apply for a loan, lenders usually require documents to prove that your income is high enough to repay the loan. For example, a lender might ask to see copies of your most recent pay stubs, income tax filings, and bank account statements. In a "no-doc" or "low-doc" loan, the lender doesn't require you to bring proof of your income, but you will usually have to pay a higher interest rate or extra fees to get the loan. Lenders generally charge more for no-doc/low-doc loans.

Interest-rate caps

An interest-rate cap places a limit on the amount your interest rate can increase. Interest caps come in two versions:

- *A periodic adjustment cap*, which limits the amount the interest rate can adjust up or down from one adjustment period to the next after the first adjustment, and

- *A lifetime cap*, which limits the interest-rate increase over the life of the loan. By law, virtually all ARMs must have a lifetime cap.

Periodic adjustment caps

Let's suppose you have an ARM with a periodic adjustment interest-rate cap of 2%. However, at the first adjustment, the index rate has risen 3%. The following example shows what happens.

Examples in This Handbook

All examples in this handbook are based on a $200,000 loan amount and a 30-year term. Payment amounts in the examples do not include taxes, insurance, condominium or homeowner association fees, or similar items. These amounts can be a significant part of your monthly payment.

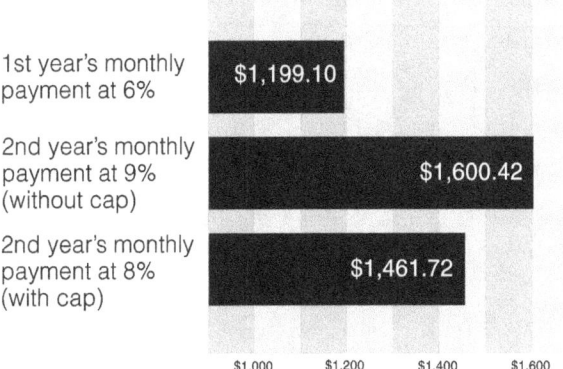

1st year's monthly payment at 6% — $1,199.10

2nd year's monthly payment at 9% (without cap) — $1,600.42

2nd year's monthly payment at 8% (with cap) — $1,461.72

$1,000 $1,200 $1,400 $1,600

Difference in 2nd year between payment with cap and payment without = $138.70 per month

In this example, because of the cap on your loan, your monthly payment in year 2 is $138.70 per month lower than it would be without the cap, saving you $1,664.40 over the year.

Some ARMs allow a larger rate change at the first adjustment and then apply a periodic adjustment cap to all future adjustments.

A drop in interest rates does not always lead to a drop in your monthly payments. With some ARMs that have interest-rate caps, the cap may hold your rate and payment below what it would have been if the change in the index rate had been fully applied. The increase in the interest that was not imposed because of the rate cap might carry over to future rate adjustments. This is called *carryover*. So, at the next adjustment date, your payment might increase even though the index rate has stayed the same or declined.

The following example shows how carryovers work. Suppose the index on your ARM increased 3% during the first year.

Because this ARM limits rate increases to 2% at any one time, the rate is adjusted by only 2%, to 8% for the second year. However, the remaining 1% increase in the index carries over to the next time the lender can adjust rates. So, when the lender adjusts the interest rate for the third year, even if there has been no change in the index during the second year, the rate still increases by 1%, to 9%.

1st year at 6%

If index rises 3%, to 9%, 2nd year with 2% rate cap at 8%

If index stays the same for the 3rd year, at 9%

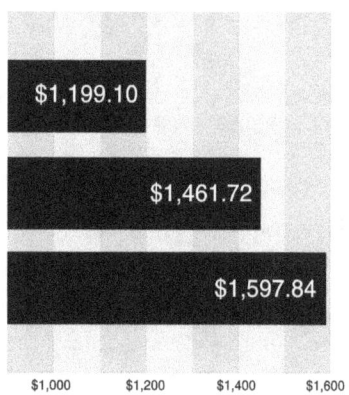

1st year at 6%	$1,199.10
If index rises 3%, to 9%, 2nd year with 2% rate cap at 8%	$1,461.72
If index stays the same for the 3rd year, at 9%	$1,597.84

$1,000 $1,200 $1,400 $1,600

In general, the rate on your loan can go up at any scheduled adjustment date when the lender's standard ARM rate (the index plus the margin) is higher than the rate you are paying before that adjustment.

Lifetime caps

The next example shows how a lifetime rate cap would affect your loan. Let's say that your ARM starts out with a 6% rate and the loan has a 6% lifetime cap—that is, the rate can never exceed 12%. Suppose the index rate increases 1% in each of the next 9 years. With a 6% overall cap, your payment would never exceed $1,998.84—compared with the $2,409.11 that it would have reached in the tenth year without a cap.

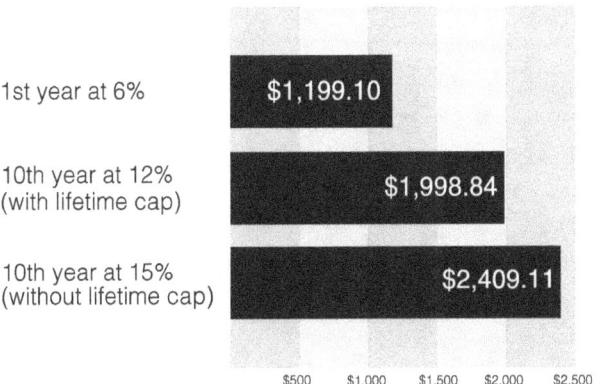

1st year at 6% — $1,199.10

10th year at 12% (with lifetime cap) — $1,998.84

10th year at 15% (without lifetime cap) — $2,409.11

$500 $1,000 $1,500 $2,000 $2,500

Payment caps

In addition to interest-rate caps, many ARMs—including payment-option ARMs (discussed on page 16)—limit, or cap, the amount your monthly payment may increase at the time of each adjustment. For example, if your loan has a payment cap of 7½%, your monthly payment won't increase more than 7½% over your previous payment, even if interest rates rise more. For example, if your monthly payment in year 1 of your mortgage was $1,000, it could only go up to $1,075 in year 2 (7½% of $1,000 is an additional $75). Any interest you don't pay because of the payment cap will be added to the balance of your loan. A payment cap can limit the increase to your monthly payments but also can add to the amount you owe on the loan. (This is called *negative amortization*, a term explained on page 22.)

Let's assume that your rate changes in the first year by 2 percentage points, but your payments can increase no more than 7½% in any 1 year. The following graph shows what your monthly payments would look like.

While your monthly payment will be only $1,289.03 for the

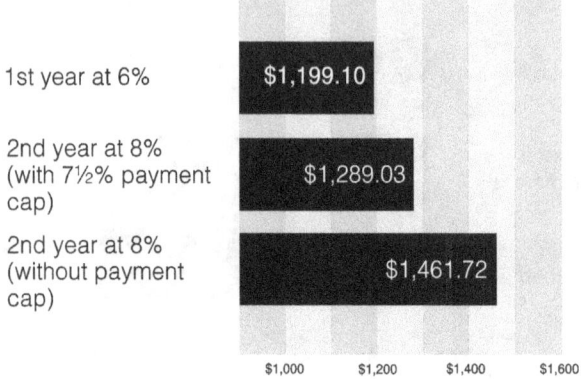

1st year at 6% — $1,199.10

2nd year at 8% (with 7½% payment cap) — $1,289.03

2nd year at 8% (without payment cap) — $1,461.72

$1,000 $1,200 $1,400 $1,600

Difference in monthly payment = $172.69

second year, the difference of $172.69 each month will be added to the balance of your loan and will lead to negative amortization.

Some ARMs with payment caps do not have periodic interest-rate caps. In addition, as explained below, most payment-option ARMs have a built-in recalculation period, usually every 5 years. At that point, your payment will be recalculated (lenders use the term *recast*) based on the remaining term of the loan. If you have a 30-year loan and you are at the end of year 5, your payment will be recalculated for the remaining 25 years. The payment cap does not apply to this adjustment. If your loan balance has increased, or if interest rates have risen faster than your payments, your payments could go up a lot.

Types of ARMs

Hybrid ARMs

Hybrid ARMs often are advertised as 3/1 or 5/1 ARMs—you might also see ads for 7/1 or 10/1 ARMs. These loans are a mix—or a hybrid—of a fixed-rate period and an adjustable-rate period. The interest rate is fixed for the first few years of these loans—for example, for 5 years in a 5/1 ARM. After that, the rate may adjust annually (the 1 in the 5/1 example), until the loan is paid off. In the case of 3/1 or 5/1 ARMs:

■ the first number tells you how long the fixed interest-rate period will be, and

■ the second number tells you how often the rate will adjust after the initial period.

You may also see ads for 2/28 or 3/27 ARMs—the first number tells you how many years the fixed interest-rate period will be, and the second number tells you the number of years the rates on the loan will be adjustable. Some 2/28 and 3/27 mortgages adjust every 6 months, not annually.

Interest-only (I-O) ARMs

An interest-only (I-O) ARM payment plan allows you to *pay only the interest* for a specified number of years, typically for 3 to 10 years. This allows you to have smaller monthly payments for a period. After that, your monthly payment will increase—even if interest rates stay the same—because you must start paying back the principal as well as the interest each month.

For some I-O loans, the interest rate adjusts during the I-O period as well.

For example, if you take out a 30-year mortgage loan with a 5-year I-O payment period, you can pay only interest for 5 years and then you must pay both the principal and interest over the next 25 years. Because you begin to pay back the principal, your payments increase after year 5, even if the rate stays the same. Keep in mind that the longer the I-O period, the higher your monthly payments will be after the I-O period ends.

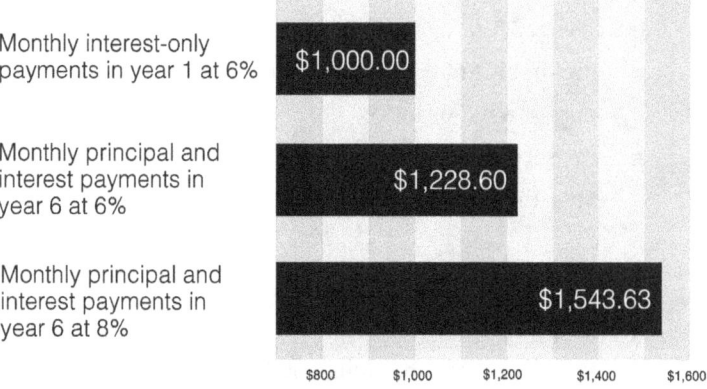

Monthly interest-only payments in year 1 at 6% — $1,000.00

Monthly principal and interest payments in year 6 at 6% — $1,228.60

Monthly principal and interest payments in year 6 at 8% — $1,543.63

$800 $1,000 $1,200 $1,400 $1,600

Payment-option ARMs

A payment-option ARM is an adjustable-rate mortgage that allows you to choose among several payment options each month. The options typically include the following:

■ *a traditional payment of principal and interest,* which reduces the amount you owe on your mortgage. These payments are based on a set loan term, such as a 15-, 30-, or 40-year payment schedule.

- *an interest-only payment,* which pays the interest but does not reduce the amount you owe on your mortgage as you make your payments.

- *a minimum (or limited) payment* that may be less than the amount of interest due that month and may not reduce the amount you owe on your mortgage. If you choose this option, the amount of any interest you do not pay will be added to the principal of the loan, **increasing the amount you owe and your future monthly payments**, and increasing the amount of interest you will pay over the life of the loan. In addition, if you pay only the minimum payment in the last few years of the loan, you may owe a larger payment at the end of the loan term, called a *balloon payment.*

The interest rate on a payment-option ARM is typically very low for the first few months (for example, 2% for the first 1 to 3 months). After that, the interest rate usually rises to a rate closer to that of other mortgage loans. Your payments during the first year are based on the initial low rate, meaning that if you only make the minimum payment each month, it will not reduce the amount you owe and it may not cover the interest due. The unpaid interest is added to the amount you owe on the mortgage, and your loan balance increases. This is called *negative amortization.* This means that even after making many payments, you could owe more than you did at the beginning of the loan. Also, as interest rates go up, your payments are likely to go up.

Payment-option ARMs have a built-in recalculation period, usually every 5 years. At this point, your payment will be recalculated (or "recast") based on the remaining term of the loan. If you have a 30-year loan and you are at the end of year 5, your payment will be recalculated for the remaining 25 years. If your loan balance has increased because you have made only minimum payments, or if interest rates have risen faster than your payments, your payments will increase each time your loan is recast. At each recast, your new minimum payment will be a fully amortizing payment and any payment cap will not apply. This means that your monthly payment can increase a lot at each recast.

Lenders may recalculate your loan payments before the recast period if the amount of principal you owe grows beyond a set limit, say 110% or 125% of your original mortgage amount. For example, suppose you made only minimum payments on your $200,000 mortgage and had any unpaid interest added to your balance. If the balance grew to $250,000 (125% of $200,000), your lender would recalculate your payments so that you would pay off the loan over the remaining term. It is likely that your payments would go up substantially.

More information on interest-only and payment-option ARMs is available in a Federal Reserve Board brochure, *Interest-Only Mortgage Payments and Payment-Option ARMs—Are They for You?* (available online at www.federalreserve.gov/ consumerinfo/mortgages.htm).

Consumer cautions

Discounted interest rates

Many lenders offer more than one type of ARM. Some lenders offer an ARM with an initial rate that is lower than their fully indexed ARM rate (that is, lower than the sum of the index plus the margin). Such rates—called discounted rates, start rates, or teaser rates—are often combined with large initial loan fees, sometimes called *points*, and with higher rates after the initial discounted rate expires.

Your lender or broker may offer you a choice of loans that may include "discount points" or a "discount fee." You may choose to pay these points or fees in return for a lower interest rate. But keep in mind that the lower interest rate may only last until the first adjustment.

If a lender offers you a loan with a discount rate, don't assume that means that the loan is a good one for you. You should carefully consider whether you will be able to afford higher payments in later years when the discount expires and the rate is adjusted.

Here is an example of how a discounted initial rate might work. Let's assume that the lender's fully indexed 1-year ARM rate (index rate plus margin) is currently 6%; the monthly payment for the first year would be $1,199.10. But your lender is offering an ARM with a discounted initial rate of 4% for the first year. With the 4% rate, your first-year's monthly payment would be $954.83.

With a discounted ARM, your initial payment will probably remain at $954.83 for only a limited time—and any savings during the discount period may be offset by higher payments over the remaining life of the mortgage. If you are considering a discount ARM, be sure to compare future payments with those for a fully indexed ARM. In fact, if you buy a home or refinance using a deeply discounted initial rate, you run the risk of payment shock, negative amortization, or prepayment penalties or conversion fees.

Payment shock

Payment shock may occur if your mortgage payment rises sharply at a rate adjustment. Let's see what would happen in the second year if the rate on your discounted 4% ARM were to rise to the 6% fully indexed rate.

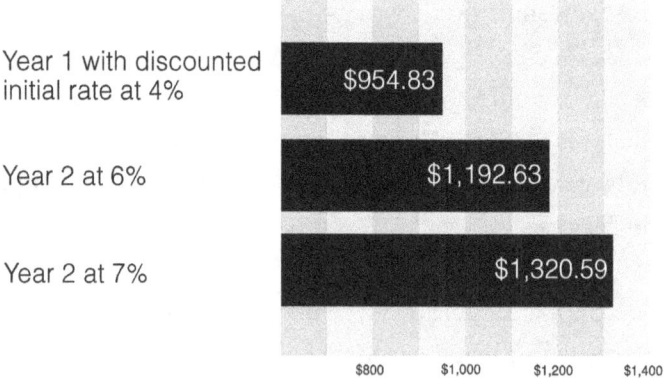

Year 1 with discounted initial rate at 4% — $954.83

Year 2 at 6% — $1,192.63

Year 2 at 7% — $1,320.59

$800 $1,000 $1,200 $1,400

As the example shows, even if the index rate were to stay the same, your monthly payment would go up from $954.83 to $1,192.63 in the second year.

Suppose that the index rate increases 1% in 1 year and the ARM rate rises to 7%. Your payment in the second year would be $1,320.59.

That's an increase of $365.76 in your monthly payment. You can see what might happen if you choose an ARM because of a low initial rate without considering whether you will be able to afford future payments.

If you have an interest-only ARM, payment shock can also occur when the interest-only period ends. Or, if you have a payment-option ARM, payment shock can happen when the loan is recast.

The following example compares several different loans over the first 7 years of their terms; the payments shown are for years 1, 6, and 7 of the mortgage, assuming you make interest-only payments or minimum payments. The main point is that, depending on the terms and conditions of your mortgage and changes in interest rates, ARM payments can change quite a bit over the life of the loan—so while you could save money in the first few years of an ARM, you could also face much higher payments in the future.

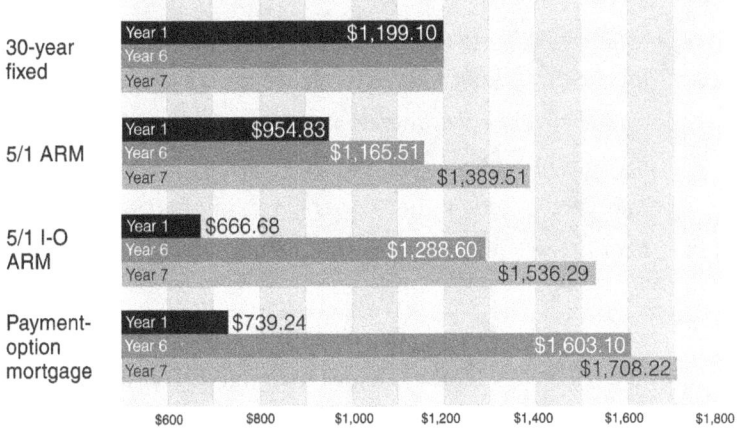

Negative amortization—When you owe more money than you borrowed

Negative amortization means that the amount you owe increases even when you make all your required payments on time. It occurs whenever your monthly mortgage payments are not large enough to pay all of the interest due on your mortgage—meaning the unpaid interest is added to the principal on your mortgage and you will owe more than you originally borrowed. This can happen because you are making only minimum payments on a payment-option mortgage or because your loan has a payment cap.

For example, suppose you have a $200,000, 30-year payment-option ARM with a 2% rate for the first 3 months and a 6% rate for the remaining 9 months of the year. Your minimum payment for the year is $739.24, as shown in the previous graph. However, once the 6% rate is applied to your loan balance, you are no longer covering the interest costs. If you continue to make minimum payments on this loan, your loan balance at the end of the first year of your mortgage would be $201,118—or $1,118 more than you originally borrowed.

Because payment caps limit only the amount of payment increases, and not interest-rate increases, payments sometimes do not cover all the interest due on your loan. This means that the unpaid interest is automatically added to your debt, and interest may be charged on that amount. You might owe the lender more later in the loan term than you did at the beginning.

A payment cap limits the increase in your monthly payment by deferring some of the interest. Eventually, you would have to repay the higher remaining loan balance at the interest rate then in effect. When this happens, there may be a substantial increase in your monthly payment.

Some mortgages include a cap on negative amortization. The cap typically limits the total amount you can owe to 110% to 125% of the original loan amount. When you reach that point, the lender will set the monthly payment amounts to fully repay the loan over the remaining term. Your payment cap will not apply, and your payments could be substantially higher. You may limit negative amortization by voluntarily increasing your monthly payment.

Be sure you know whether the ARM you are considering can have negative amortization.

Home Prices, Home Equity, and ARMs

Sometimes home prices rise rapidly, allowing people to quickly build equity in their homes. This can make some people think that even if the rate and payments on their ARM get too high, they can avoid those higher payments by refinancing their loan or, in the worst case, selling their home. It's important to remember that home prices do not always go up quickly—they may increase a little or remain the same, and sometimes they fall. If housing prices fall, your home may not be worth as much as you owe on the mortgage. Also, you may find it difficult to refinance your loan to get a lower monthly payment or rate. Even if home prices stay the same, if your loan lets you make minimum payments (see *payment-option ARMs* on page 16), you may owe your lender more on your mortgage than you could get from selling your home.

Prepayment penalties and conversion

If you get an ARM, you may decide later that you don't want to risk any increases in the interest rate and payment amount. When you are considering an ARM, ask for information about any extra fees you would have to pay if you pay off the loan early by refinancing or selling your home, and whether you would be able to convert your ARM to a fixed-rate mortgage.

Prepayment penalties

Some ARMs, including interest-only and payment-option ARMs, may require you to pay special fees or penalties if you refinance or pay off the ARM early (usually within the first 3 to 5 years of the loan). Some loans have *hard prepayment penalties*, meaning that you will pay an extra fee or penalty if you pay off the loan during the penalty period for any reason (because you refinance or sell your home, for example). Other loans have *soft prepayment penalties*, meaning that you will pay an extra fee or penalty only if you refinance the loan, but you will not pay a penalty if you sell your home. Also, some loans may have prepayment penalties even if you make only a partial prepayment.

Prepayment penalties can be several thousand dollars. For example, suppose you have a 3/1 ARM with an initial rate of 6%. At the end of year 2 you decide to refinance and pay off your original loan. At the time of refinancing, your balance is $194,936. If your loan has a prepayment penalty of 6 months' interest on the remaining balance, you would owe about $5,850.

Sometimes there is a trade-off between having a prepayment penalty and having lower origination fees or lower interest rates.

The lender may be willing to reduce or eliminate a prepayment penalty based on the amount you pay in loan fees or on the interest rate in the loan contract.

If you have a hybrid ARM—such as a 2/28 or 3/27 ARM—be sure to compare the prepayment penalty period with the ARM's first adjustment period. For example, if you have a 2/28 ARM that has a rate and payment adjustment after the second year, but the prepayment penalty is in effect for the first 5 years of the loan, it may be costly to refinance when the first adjustment is made.

Most mortgages let you make additional principal payments with your monthly payment. In most cases, this is not considered prepayment, and there usually is no penalty for these extra amounts. Check with your lender to make sure there is no penalty if you think you might want to make this type of additional principal prepayment.

Conversion fees

Your agreement with the lender may include a clause that lets you convert the ARM to a fixed-rate mortgage at designated times. When you convert, the new rate is generally set using a formula given in your loan documents.

The interest rate or up-front fees may be somewhat higher for a convertible ARM. Also, a convertible ARM may require a fee at the time of conversion.

Graduated-payment or stepped-rate loans

Some fixed-rate loans start with one rate for 1 or 2 years and then change to another rate for the remaining term of the loan. While these are not ARMs, your payment will go up according to the terms of your contract. Talk with your lender or broker and read the information provided to you to make sure you understand when and by how much the payment will change.

Where to get information

Disclosures from lenders

You should receive information in writing about each ARM program you are interested in before you have paid a nonrefundable fee. It is important that you read this information and ask the lender or broker about anything you don't understand—index rates, margins, caps, and other ARM features such as negative amortization. After you have applied for a loan, you will get more information from the lender about your loan, including the APR, a payment schedule, and whether the loan has a prepayment penalty.

The APR is the cost of your credit as a yearly rate. It takes into account interest, points paid on the loan, any fees paid to the lender for making the loan, and any mortgage insurance premiums you may have to pay. You can compare APRs on similar ARMs (for example, compare APRs on a 5/1 and a 3/1 ARM) to determine which loan will cost you less in the long term, but you should keep in mind that because the interest rate for an ARM can change, APRs on ARMs cannot be compared directly to APRs for fixed-rate mortgages.

You may want to talk with financial advisers, housing counselors, and other trusted advisers. Contact a local housing counseling agency, call the U.S. Department of Housing and Urban Development toll-free at 800-569-4287, or visit www.hud.gov/offices/hsg/sfh/hcc/hccprof14.cfm to find an agency near you.

Also, see our *Where to go for help* on page A6, for a list of federal agencies that can provide more information and assistance.

Newspapers and the Internet

When buying a home or refinancing your existing mortgage, remember to shop around. Compare costs and terms, and negotiate for the best deal. Your local newspaper and the Internet are good places to start shopping for a loan. You can usually find information on interest rates and points for several lenders. Since rates and points can change daily, you'll want to check information sources often when shopping for a home loan.

The Mortgage Shopping Worksheet on page 2 may also help you. Take it with you when you speak to each lender or broker, and write down the information you obtain. Don't be afraid to make lenders and brokers compete with each other for your business by letting them know that you are shopping for the best deal.

Advertisements

Any initial information you receive about mortgages probably will come from advertisements or mail solicitations from builders, real estate brokers, mortgage brokers, and lenders. Although this information can be helpful, keep in mind that these are marketing materials—the ads and mailings are designed to make the mortgage look as attractive as possible. These ads may play up low initial interest rates and monthly payments, without emphasizing that those rates and payments could increase substantially later. So, get all the facts.

Any ad for an ARM that shows an initial interest rate should also show how long the rate is in effect and the APR on the loan. If the APR is much higher than the initial rate, your payments may increase a lot after the introductory period, even if interest rates stay the same.

Choosing a mortgage may be the most important financial decision you will make. You are entitled to have all the information you need to make the right decision. Don't hesitate to ask questions about ARM features when you talk to lenders, mortgage brokers, real estate agents, sellers, and your attorney, and keep asking until you get clear and complete answers.

Glossary

Adjustable-rate mortgage (ARM)

A mortgage that does not have a fixed interest rate. The rate changes during the life of the loan based on movements in an index rate, such as the rate for Treasury securities or the Cost of Funds Index. ARMs usually offer a lower initial interest rate than fixed-rate loans. The interest rate fluctuates over the life of the loan based on market conditions, but the loan agreement generally sets maximum and minimum rates. When interest rates increase, generally your loan payments increase; and when interest rates decrease, your monthly payments may decrease.

Annual percentage rate (APR)

The cost of credit expressed as a yearly rate. For closed-end credit, such as car loans or mortgages, the APR includes the interest rate, points, broker fees, and other credit charges that the borrower is required to pay. An APR, or an equivalent rate, is not used in leasing agreements.

Balloon payment

A large extra payment that may be charged at the end of a mortgage loan or lease.

Buydown

When the seller pays an amount to the lender so that the lender can give you a lower rate and lower payments, usually for an initial period in an ARM. The seller may increase the sales price to cover the cost of the buydown. Buydowns can occur in all types of mortgages, not just ARMs.

Cap, interest rate

A limit on the amount that your interest rate can increase. The two types of interest rate caps are *periodic adjustment caps* and *lifetime caps*. *Periodic adjustment caps* limit the interest-rate increase from one adjustment period to the next. *Lifetime caps* limit the interest-rate increase over the life of the loan. All adjustable-rate mortgages have an overall cap.

Cap, payment

A limit on the amount that your monthly mortgage payment on a loan may change, usually a percentage of the loan. The limit can be applied each time the payment changes or during the life of the mortgage. Payment caps may lead to negative amortization because they do not limit the amount of interest the lender is earning.

Conversion clause

A provision in some ARMs that allows you to change the ARM to a fixed-rate loan at some point during the term. Conversion is usually allowed at the end of the first adjustment period. At the time of the conversion, the new fixed rate is generally set at one of the rates then prevailing for fixed-rate mortgages. The conversion feature may be available at extra cost.

Discounted initial rate (also known as a start rate or teaser rate)

In an ARM with a discounted initial rate, the lender offers you a lower rate and lower payments for part of the mortgage term (usually for 1, 3, or 5 years). After the discount period, the ARM rate will probably go up depending on the index rate. Discounts can occur in all types of mortgages, not just ARMs.

Equity

In housing markets, equity is the difference between the fair market value of the home and the outstanding balance on your mortgage plus any outstanding home equity loans. In vehicle leasing markets, equity is the positive difference between the trade-in or market value of your vehicle and the loan payoff amount.

Hybrid ARM

These ARMs are a mix—or a hybrid—of a fixed-rate period and an adjustable-rate period. The interest rate is fixed for the first several years of the loan; after that period, the rate can adjust annually. For example, hybrid ARMs can be advertised as 3/1 or 5/1—the first number tells you how long the fixed interest-rate period will be and the second number tells you how often the rate will adjust after the initial period. For example, a 3/1 loan has a fixed rate for the first 3 years and then the rate adjusts once each year beginning in year 4.

Index

The economic indicator used to calculate interest-rate adjustments for adjustable-rate mortgages or other adjustable-rate loans. The index rate can increase or decrease at any time. *See also* the chart on page 8, *Selected index rates for ARMs over an 11-year period*, for examples of common indexes that have changed in the past.

Interest

The rate used to determine the cost of borrowing money, usually stated as a percentage and as an annual rate.

Interest-only (I-O) ARM

Interest-only ARMs allow you to pay only the interest for a specified number of years, typically between 3 and 10 years. This arrangement allows you to have smaller monthly payments for a prescribed period. After that period, your monthly payment will increase — even if interest rates stay the same — because you must start paying back the principal and the interest each month. For some I-O loans, the interest rate adjusts during the I-O period as well.

Margin

The number of percentage points the lender adds to the index rate to calculate the interest rate of an adjustable-rate mortgage (ARM) at each adjustment.

Negative amortization

Occurs when the monthly payments in an adjustable-rate mortgage loan do not cover all the interest owed. The interest that is not paid in the monthly payment is added to the loan balance. This means that even after making many payments, you could owe more than you did at the beginning of the loan. Negative amortization can occur when an ARM has a payment cap that results in monthly payments that are not high enough to cover the interest due or when the minimum payments are set at an amount lower than the amount you owe in interest.

Payment-option ARM

An ARM that allows the borrower to choose among several payment options each month. The options typically include (1) a traditional amortizing payment of principal and interest, (2) an interest-only payment, or (3) a minimum (or limited) payment that may be less than the amount of interest due that month. If the borrower chooses the minimum-payment option, the amount of any interest that is not paid will be added to the principal of the loan. *See also* Negative amortization on page A4.

Points (also called discount points)

One point is equal to 1 percent of the principal amount of a mortgage loan. For example, if the mortgage is $200,000, one point equals $2,000. Lenders frequently charge points in both fixed-rate and adjustable-rate mortgages to cover loan origination costs or to provide additional compensation to the lender or broker. These points usually are paid at closing and may be paid by the borrower or the home seller, or may be split between them. In some cases, the money needed to pay points can be borrowed (incorporated in the loan amount), but doing so will increase the loan amount and the total costs. Discount points (also called discount fees) are points that the borrower voluntarily chooses to pay in return for a lower interest rate.

Prepayment penalty

Extra fees that may be due if you pay off your loan early by refinancing the loan or by selling the home. The penalty is usually limited to the first 3 to 5 years of the loan's term. If your loan includes a prepayment penalty, make sure you understand the cost. Compare the length of the prepayment penalty period with the first adjustment period of the ARM to see if refinancing is cost-effective before the loan first adjusts. Some loans may have a prepayment penalty even if you make a partial prepayment. Ask the lender for a loan without a prepayment penalty and the cost of that loan.

Principal

The amount of money borrowed or the amount still owed on a loan.

Where to go for help

For additional information or to file a complaint about a bank, savings and loan, credit union, or other financial institution, contact one of the following federal agencies, depending on the type of institution.

Regulatory Agency	Regulated Entity(ies)	Telephone/Website
Federal Reserve Consumer Help P.O. Box 1200 Minneapolis, MN 55480	Federally insured state-chartered bank members of the Federal Reserve System	(888) 851-1920 www.federalreservecon-sumerhelp.gov
Consumer Financial Protection Bureau (CFPB) P.O. Box 4503 Iowa City, IA 52244	Insured depository institutions and credit unions (and their affiliates) with assets greater than $10 billion, and nondepository institutions such as mortgage originators, mortgage brokers and servicers, larger participants of other financial services products, private education loan providers, and payday lenders	(855) 411-2372 www.consumerfinance.gov
Office of the Comptroller of the Currency (OCC) Customer Assistance Unit 1301 McKinney Street Suite 3450 Houston, TX 77010	National banks and federally chartered savings banks/associations	(800) 613-6743 www.occ.treas.gov www.helpwithmybank.gov
Federal Deposit Insurance Corporation (FDIC) Consumer Response Center 1100 Walnut Street, Box #11 Kansas City, MO 64106	Federally insured state-chartered banks that are not members of the Federal Reserve System	(877) ASK-FDIC or (877) 275-3342 www.fdic.gov www.fdic.gov/consumers

Regulatory Agency	Regulated Entity(ies)	Telephone/Website
Federal Housing Finance Agency (FHFA) Consumer Communications Constitution Center 400 7th Street, S.W. Washington, DC 20024	Fannie Mae, Freddie Mac, and the Federal Home Loan Banks	(202) 649-3811 www.fhfa.gov www.fhfa.gov/Default. aspx?Page=369
National Credit Union Administration (NCUA) Consumer Assistance 1775 Duke Street Alexandria, VA 22314-3428	Federally chartered credit unions	(800) 755-1030 www.ncua.gov www.mycreditunion.gov
Federal Trade Commission (FTC) Consumer Response Center 600 Pennsylvania Avenue, N.W. Washington, DC 20580	Finance companies, retail stores, auto dealers, mortgage companies and other lenders, and credit bureaus	(877) FTC-HELP or (877) 382-4357 www.ftc.gov www.ftc.gov/bcp
Securities and Exchange Commission (SEC) Complaint Center 100 F Street, N.E. Washington, DC 20549-0213	Brokerage firms, mutual fund companies, and investment advisers	(202) 551-6551 www.sec.gov www.sec.gov/complaint/ question.shtml
Farm Credit Administration Office of Congressional and Public Affairs 1501 Farm Credit Drive McLean, VA 22102-5090	Agricultural lenders	(703) 883-4056 www.fca.gov
Small Business Administration (SBA) Consumer Affairs 409 3rd Street, S.W. Washington, DC 20416	Small business lenders	(800) U-ASK-SBA or (800) 827-5722 www.sba.gov

Regulatory Agency	Regulated Entity(ies)	Telephone/Website
Commodity Futures Trading Commission (CFTC) 1155 21st Street, N.W. Washington, DC 20581	Commodity brokers, commodity trading advisers, commodity pools, and introducing brokers	(866) 366-2382 www.cftc.gov/Consumer-Protection
U.S. Department of Justice (DOJ) Criminal Division 950 Pennsylvania Avenue, N.W. Washington, DC 20530	Fair lending and fair housing issues	(202) 514-3301 www.justice.gov/criminal
Department of Housing and Urban Development (HUD) Office of Fair Housing/ Equal Opportunity 451 7th Street, S.W. Washington, DC 20410	Fair lending and fair housing issues	(800) 669-9777 www.hud.gov/complaints

More resources

Looking for the Best Mortgage—Shop, Compare, Negotiate
(at www.federalreserve.gov/pubs/mortgage/mortb_1.htm)

Interest-Only Mortgage Payments and Payment-Option ARMs—Are They for You?
(at www.federalreserve.gov/pubs/mortgage_interestonly/)

A Consumer's Guide to Mortgage Lock-Ins
(at www.federalreserve.gov/pubs/lockins/default.htm)

A Consumer's Guide to Mortgage Settlement Costs
(at www.federalreserve.gov/pubs/settlement/default.htm)

Know Before You Go . . .To Get a Mortgage: A Guide to Mortgage Products and a Glossary of Lending Terms
(at www.bos.frb.org/consumer/knowbeforeyougo/mortgage/mortgage.pdf)

Partners Online Mortgage Calculator
(at www.frbatlanta.org/partnerssoftwareonline/dsp_main.cfm)

For more information on mortgage and other financial topics, including interactive calculators, visit www.federalreserve.gov/consumerinfo.